This book is due for return on or before the last date shown below.

LIVES IN CRISIS

The Great Depression

R. G. GRANT

HODDER
Wayland

an imprint of Hodder Children's Books

Cover and page 1:
A farming family in the USA, on the move seeking a new place to live and work, 1938.

Acknowledgements

The Author and Publishers thank the following for their permission to reproduce photographs: Corbis: pages 4 (Bettmann), 5 (Bettmann), 6, 7 (Bettmann), 9 (Hulton-Deutsch Collection), 10t (Hulton-Deutsch Collection), 11, 18, 20 (Minnesota Historical Society), 21 (Minnesota Historical Society), 24 (Horace Bristol), 26 (Bettmann), 29 (E. O. Hoppé), 35 (Bettmann), 36 (E. O. Hoppé), 37 (Underwood and Underwood), 38 (Bettmann), 39, 41, 42, 43 (Bettmann), 45 (Hulton-Deutsch Collection), 46 (Bettmann), 48 (Bettmann), 52t, 52b, 56 (Bettmann), 59 (James P. Blair); Peter Newark's Historical Pictures: cover and pages 1, 8, 10b, 12, 22, 25, 27, 33, 35b, 40, 49, 51; Popperfoto: cover and pages 3, 15, 16, 17, 23, 28, 31, 47, 55, 57t, 57b.

CONTENTS

Queueing outside a soup kitchen in Chicago, November 1930.

A WORLD GONE WRONG

On 28 July 1932, armed American troops were sent on to the streets of Washington DC. About 600 soldiers, including infantry with bayonets fixed and cavalry with sabres drawn, under the command of some of the country's highest-ranking officers, had orders to clear the American capital of a ragtag body of unemployed workers who had set up camp there. The protest of these men, who called themselves the Bonus Army, had dramatized the anger and hopelessness felt by millions of people, in the USA and across the world, as their lives were shattered by the impact of the worst economic crisis in modern history: the Great Depression.

In charge of the troops sent in to deal with the Bonus Army were Chief of Staff, General Douglas MacArthur (left) and his second in command, Colonel Dwight D. Eisenhower.

Beginning in 1929, businesses and farms had gone bankrupt, banks had collapsed, factories had closed down and the flow of world trade had shrunk to a trickle. The result was mass unemployment. By 1932, an estimated 12 million Americans were without a job – about one in four of the workforce. In Britain some 3 million people were out of work, and in Germany the situation was even worse, with about one worker in three unemployed. Inevitably, unemployment brought poverty in its wake. Many people went hungry, especially in the USA, where there was little or no financial support for the unemployed. Some Americans were convinced that the poorest of their fellow citizens were literally dying of starvation.

The Bonus Army

The Bonus Army was made up of war veterans – men who had fought for the USA in the First World War. Their specific grievance focused on a 'bonus' that the US government had granted to veterans in 1924, in recognition of their service to their country. The terms of the grant meant that the men would not have access to all the money owed them – around $1,000 – until 1945. As the Depression hit home, unemployed veterans had begun to campaign for the bonus to be paid immediately in cash.

In the early summer of 1932, more than 20,000 veterans assembled in Washington. They travelled from all over the USA – the central core came from Oregon – and their highly publicized progress to Washington focused nationwide interest on their cause. They were housed in disused buildings in the capital or on empty land at Anacostia Flats, where they built themselves shacks

The Bonus Army camp at Anacostia Flats in Washington DC. The protesters intended to stay until their demands were met.

A bitter man

A Bonus Army veteran's wife described what drove him to take part in the Washington protest in 1932:

'My husband was very bitter. That's just puttin' it mild. He was an intelligent man. He couldn't see why as wealthy a country as this is, that there was any sense in so many people starving to death.'
(Quoted in Terkel, *Hard Times*)

President Herbert Hoover speaks to the press.

from bits of timber and cans. About 700 wives and 400 children came to share this makeshift accommodation with the unemployed veterans.

The protesters intended to stay in Washington until the bonus was paid. But the US president, Herbert Hoover, and the US Senate were resolutely opposed to paying the money. Hoover was in general against the idea of giving government cash to the unemployed. In an attempt to defuse the situation, the US Congress voted to pay the veterans' rail fares so they could go home. But by the last week in July 10,000 protesters were still in Washington and their mood was turning ugly.

On the morning of 28 July fighting broke out between veterans and police; two veterans were shot dead. At this point Hoover called out the troops. The clearing of the camp at Anacostia Flats was swift and spectacular. The area was

Give us food and work

An unemployed American poured out his anger in an anonymous letter to President Hoover at the height of the Depression:

'Could we not have employment and food to eat? Why should we have ... foodless days ... and our children have school-less days and shoeless days, and the land full of plenty and banks bursting with money. Why does everything have exceptional value except the human being? ... Why not end the Depression? Have you not a heart?'
(Quoted in McElvaine, *Down and Out in the Great Depression*)

blanketed in tear gas as the soldiers moved in and the flimsy shacks went up in flames. Routed, the Bonus Army protesters drifted away.

The use of troops to drive out protesters outraged much of public opinion. The Bonus Army enjoyed considerable public sympathy because they were posing wider questions that people thought needed an answer. Where had mass unemployment come from and what could be done to end it? Why was there poverty and hunger when farmland and factories capable of producing food and goods in large quantities were lying idle? There was a widespread feeling that something had gone badly wrong with the world, but no one knew quite why, or what should be done about it.

This book will describe the events that led up to the Depression, the impact that the crisis had on people's lives, and the radical attempts that were made to find a solution. It will show how the shock of the Depression has remained an influence on attitudes down to the present day.

Bonus Army shacks on fire, July 1932: images such as this helped turn public opinion against President Hoover.

BOOM AND BUST

The Great Depression began at the end of the 1920s, but the roots of the crisis went back to the First World War (1914-18). As well as costing 10 million people their lives, the war badly disrupted the world economy. Before 1914, the complex business of international trade and finance had been carried out in a generally stable and predictable way. It was not a 'golden age': poverty was widespread, working conditions were hard for most people and occasional economic downturns brought short periods of high unemployment. But from the point of view of businessmen and industrialists, at least, the system had worked well.

After the war, most people expected a gradual return to pre-war conditions – a return to what Americans called 'normalcy'. Yet this proved impossible to achieve. Europe, in particular, had become a far less stable place. Germany, second only to the USA as an industrial power before 1914, was in chaos for years after the war ended. In Russia, a Bolshevik revolution in 1917 had brought the world's first communist government to

A British Labour Party poster from the 1920s highlights the fate of many soldiers who fought for their country in the First World War, only to face long-term unemployment afterwards.

YESTERDAY-THE TRENCHES TO-DAY-UNEMPLOYED

power, challenging the basic principles of the world economic and political order. In Italy, Benito Mussolini, head of the blackshirted Fascists, came to power in 1922, soon establishing a one-party dictatorship.

Signs of trouble in Europe

Before 1914 Britain had dominated world finance, but it emerged from the war heavily in debt to the USA. France, in turn, owed large sums to Britain. The two countries intended to pay their debts by taking money from defeated Germany in the form of reparations – a sort of fine for the damage caused by the war. The Germans were determined not to pay. In 1923, a confrontation between France and Germany over reparations led to a spectacular collapse in the value of the German currency. In 1918, one US dollar could be exchanged for 14 German Marks; in November 1923, the same dollar would buy 600 billion Marks. Many Germans found that their hard-earned life savings were no longer worth enough to buy a cup of coffee.

Statesmen and financial leaders worked patiently to resolve international problems and restore the confidence on which business and trade depend. Because it was now clearly the world's wealthiest country, for the first time the USA had to accept a large measure of responsibility for seeing that the global economy ran smoothly. It was the USA that arranged a deal in 1924 to resolve the crisis over reparations. US investment enabled the Germans to introduce a new Mark with real value and get their economy moving again, although the investment was in the form of short-term loans – money that could be withdrawn quickly if American banks or investors found a better use for it.

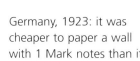

Germany, 1923: it was cheaper to paper a wall with 1 Mark notes than it was to buy wallpaper.

Trade unionists demonstrate in London during the General Strike of 1926. The strike was called in support of coalminers whose employers were demanding that they accept pay cuts.

In the USA mail order catalogues encouraged people to keep spending. This illustration was on the front of a 1927 catalogue.

By the mid-1920s, it was possible for optimists to see a return to normalcy as on the cards. But stubborn signs of trouble remained. In Britain, for example, industries such as shipbuilding and textiles had lost their overseas markets during the war and could not win them back. Throughout the 1920s Britain's industrial heartlands were stuck in a slump. There were never fewer than 1 million British unemployed in the 1920s, and often many more. In 1926, the trade union movement called a General Strike in support of coalminers, who were being forced to accept a cut in wages. Although the strike was soon called off, it showed the depth of Britain's social problems. Unemployment was also high in many other European countries in the 1920s; for example, in Norway and Denmark more than one in five workers had no job.

Boom years in the USA

The weakness of the major European economies left the world especially dependent on the health of the US economy. Fortunately, the 1920s were boom years for the USA. Many Americans were better off than ever before. The industries that most flourished were those producing new consumer goods for the mass market, above all automobiles. In 1914 there had been 500,000 cars in the USA; by 1929 there were 26 million. Another major growth area was electrical goods. Most American families bought their first radio set in the 1920s. Refrigerators, vacuum cleaners and electric irons became a feature of well-off households. The profits from the boom were flaunted in spectacular skyscrapers such as the Chrysler Building in Manhattan. Wealth also flowed out of the USA in the form of investment in Europe, especially Germany, and in Latin America. And excess cash poured into the Wall Street stock market, pushing up share prices.

Satisfaction and optimism

In his state of the nation address in December 1928, the outgoing American president, Calvin Coolidge, declared complacently:

'No Congress of the USA ever assembled, on surveying the state of the union, has met with a more pleasing prospect ... The country can regard the present with satisfaction and anticipate the future with optimism.'

The Chrysler Building in Manhattan was a spectacular symbol of the wealth and optimism of America in the 1920s. The Chrysler company made a fortune out of the boom in automobile sales.

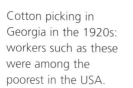

Cotton picking in Georgia in the 1920s: workers such as these were among the poorest in the USA.

But there was a downside to booming 1920s America. Although prosperity was widespread, it certainly did not include everyone. Groups such as African Americans in the rural South and miners in the Virginia coalfields suffered abject poverty throughout the 1920s. An estimated two out of five American families had barely enough money to feed and clothe themselves.

One group of Americans that did not share in the boom was small farmers and farm labourers. Along with many other parts of the world, including Canada and Australia, the USA faced a problem of agricultural overproduction. New machinery and an increase in the amount of land being farmed had greatly raised farm output, but demand for foodstuffs and other farm products had not risen as fast. Farmers came under pressure to sell their crops or animal products at ever lower prices.

The state of farming, which employed about a quarter of the American population, was a serious concern for banks. As farmers ran into financial problems, many of them raised money by mortgaging their farms or borrowing money with livestock or crops as security. If these farm loans became bad debts, many banks risked going bust. In general, Americans were too dependent on borrowed money – borrowing to buy cars, borrowing to buy shares. As long as confidence stayed high and share prices rose, this did not matter. But in 1929 the party came to an end.

A gamblers' paradise

Between 1924 and 1929, shares in the USA on average had quadrupled in value. At first the rise in share prices was largely justified by output and profits – it simply reflected the growing value of American businesses. But increasingly the 'bull market' became a speculative boom, in which people were prepared to pay ever-higher prices for shares regardless of the actual value of the companies' assets or products. It was a gamblers' paradise, in which every bet seemed a sure-fire winner, as share prices rose and rose.

Sharks and suckers

American industrialist Arthur A. Robertson, who became a millionaire in the 1920s, later wrote cynically of the period of the stock market boom:

'In 1929, it was strictly a gambling casino with loaded dice. The few sharks taking advantage of the multitude of suckers ... Everything was bought on hope.'
(Quoted in Terkel, *Hard Times*)

Small investors

In 1931, author Frederick Lewis Allen described how the fever of speculation had gripped ordinary people before the Wall Street crash:

'The rich man's chauffeur drove with his ears laid back to catch the news of an impending move in Bethlehem Steel; he held 50 shares himself on a 20-point margin [that is, bought on credit]. The window-cleaner at the broker's office paused to watch the ticker[tape], for he was thinking of converting his laboriously accumulated savings into a few shares.'
(Allen, *Only Yesterday*)

Seeing the apparent prospect of easy money to be made, more and more ordinary people were tempted to put their money into shares, many of them investing their life savings, which they could ill afford to lose. At the same time, Wall Street insiders were making fortunes through various sharp practices; for example, artificially boosting the price of shares in worthless companies in which they had a large stake.

By 1929, warning signs about the state of the US economy, and that of the world as a whole, were accumulating. Germany was already in trouble by late 1928, with unemployment rising as US investors withdrew money from abroad to put it into the stock market boom at home. In the USA, farm prices were falling and the output of some industries was weakening. Share prices wobbled in March 1929, but then went on rising in an atmosphere of feverish speculation.

The stock market collapses

On 3 September 1929 there was what experts called a 'break in the market' – a sharp fall in many share prices. No one was excessively concerned. In October, however, evidence grew that the bull market was at an end. By 19 October selling was fierce. Leading American bankers issued reassuring statements, but their calming platitudes had little effect. On Black Thursday, 24 October, the flow of selling swelled into an

Sold out

Greek-born cafe owner George Mehales was one of millions who lost everything in the Great Crash. He had been borrowing money to buy shares – buying 'on margin':

'During the last days of October, my stocks began to drop. I was gambling on the margin ... I had about 5,000 dollars invested. On that day of October 29, they told me I needed more cash to cover up. I couldn't get it. I was wiped out that day ... I considered killing myself, 'cause I had nothing left. I found out what a fool I had been. I did manage to pay my debts, by selling my cafe at rock bottom prices.' (Interview, Federal Writers' Project, Library of Congress)

overwhelming torrent that swept all before it. Panic set in at dealing rooms across the USA as people battled to unload shares that were losing value by the minute. Crowds gathered on Wall Street and rumours spread that speculators had committed suicide.

Anxious investors in Wall Street during the crash of 1929.

One share dealer described the events of 24 October as 'like a thunderclap; everyone was stunned'. In an attempt to stop the slide, President Hoover issued a reassuring statement, asserting that the USA was 'more prosperous and more industrious than ever before'. But after a brief rally, share prices plummeted again on Tuesday, 29 October, when the scenes of Black Thursday were repeated. By mid-November 1929, $30 billion had been wiped off the value of shares. Many individuals ruined by the crash had bought their now worthless stock on credit. They could not repay the loans, so the lenders – ultimately the banks – also faced heavy losses and potential ruin.

Still, many observers were convinced that the crash would be followed by business as normal. Admitting that share prices had risen too high, experts believed that the crash had 'corrected' the market. Soon shares in viable companies would start to recover their value. Sure enough, in the first three months of 1930 there was a sharp rise in prices on Wall Street. But in April they crashed again. Through the next three years, share prices simply went on going down, as each brief stock

The Wall Street crash ruined many previously well-off individuals, like the owner of this handsome automobile.

market rally was followed by a further sharp drop. By 1933, an investor who had put $10,000 into the stock market in September 1929 would have, on average, about $2,000 left. People who had bought fashionable stock such as General Motors or General Electric suffered far worse than this average.

The reason for the continued collapse of share prices in the early 1930s was not hard to find. US industry and agriculture had gone into steep decline. The boom of the 1920s had been based on confidence. With the crash, confidence had gone. Industrialists no longer believed that if they invested in new machinery or factories, they would in the future be able profitably to sell the goods that the machines and factories produced. Banks no longer felt sure that the loans they made would be repaid. Ordinary people were no longer confident that if they bought a car or furniture on credit, they would still be able to pay the instalments in a year's time. So industrialists stopped investing, banks withheld credit, and consumers stopped buying.

Crash? What crash?

Looking back, a farmer from Montana pointed out that for people like him the stock market crash was a remote event, as the majority of Americans did not hold stocks and shares:

'Everybody talks of the Crash of '29. In small towns out West, we didn't know there was a Crash. What did the stock market mean to us? Not a dang thing.' (Quoted in Badger, *The New Deal*)

The US government did its best to 'talk up' the economy. In May 1930 President Hoover assured the American people that 'we have now passed the worst, and with continued unity of effort we shall rapidly recover'. But he was wrong. Falling farm prices reached crisis point in 1930, and farmers began to go bankrupt in large numbers. More than 1,000 American banks collapsed in the course of the year. The level of unemployment in the USA was rising, by some estimates reaching about 5 million by December. The Great Depression was under way.

INTO THE ABYSS

The unprecedented nature of the Depression in the USA took time to become clear. Economists had long argued that occasional sharp downturns in the economy were inevitable – a part of the normal rhythm of economic life. The economy was supposed to right itself after a short time and resume healthy growth. This was also what most ordinary Americans at first expected. Many of them were well used to short-term unemployment. They tightened their belts and waited for jobs to start appearing again.

But the US economy stayed locked in a downward spiral. Increasingly unable to sell their goods, manufacturers cut down production. Workers lost their jobs or saw their hours cut. Either way, they had less money to spend. Better-off people, worried by the worsening economic climate and perhaps hit by the stock market crash, were also more reluctant to part with their cash, further reducing the demand for goods. Between 1929 and 1932 Westinghouse, the main manufacturer of electrical goods for American homes, lost two-thirds of its sales. Over the same period, production of automobiles halved.

People in New York fish for coins with a magnet on a string – one of many ingenious tricks devised by individuals struggling to survive in the Depression.

A poverty-stricken family take to the road in rural America, 1935. Many Americans kept cars they had bought during the 1920s boom running for the next 15 or 20 years.

Farmers face ruin

The fall in demand had a devastating effect on American agriculture. Throughout the 1920s farmers had been struggling against a tendency of prices to fall. With the onset of the Depression, the struggle was lost. Prices of products such as wheat and cotton collapsed dramatically. By 1932 it was estimated that, on average, farm products were being sold for half what it cost to produce them.

Protect your neighbours

When an American farmer fell hopelessly into debt, his property might be seized for forced sale to pay off what he owed. But local people would often join together to block the sale. A handbill distributed in a small town in the Midwest in the early 1930s read:

'Farmers and workers! Help protect your neighbors from being driven off their property. Now is the time to act ... On Friday the property of xxx is to be sold at a forced auction at the courthouse ... The Farmers' Committee has called a mass protest meeting to stop the aforementioned sale.'
(Quoted in Allen, *Since Yesterday*)

Starvation amid plenty

The point that most impressed many ordinary people during the Depression was that, while millions went hungry, farmers were suffering because they were producing food crops and meat that they could not sell. A man who was a recent immigrant to the USA in the early 1930s later recalled:

'We knew that when people didn't have the money to buy bread, the wheat was burned; if they didn't have money to buy meat, the mounds of meat were destroyed with kerosene. There was huge destruction of food in the USA at the same time that millions were starving.'
(Quoted in Hodgson, *People's Century*)

Hundreds of thousands of small farmers faced ruin. Heavily in debt, they risked having their property seized by banks hoping to recover some of the money they had loaned. The banks themselves were in a desperate state. More than 10,000 American banks failed between 1929 and 1933. When a rumour spread that a bank was in trouble, people who had deposited money there would storm the cash desks in a frantic bid to withdraw their savings. By the end of 1932 lack of confidence in banks had reached such a point that the whole banking system was on the verge of collapse.

Unemployment affects all workers

Unemployment in the USA rose from an already appalling 5 million in 1930 to an almost incredible 13 million by the end of 1932. African Americans were generally the first to be fired. In most cities, black unemployment rates were up to 60 per cent higher than those for whites. Next in line were married women, who were usually sacked when work was short – most men did not believe that married women should work anyway. But soon unemployment struck every kind of worker, from highly skilled engineers to manual labourers.

When they first became unemployed, people looked feverishly for work. The unemployed were extremely reluctant to depend

Taking action to find work, Minneapolis, Minnesota.

on benefit and craved any job that might be on offer. Queues formed on the news that hands were being taken on for work. Disillusion set in as people realized that there just was no work to be had. Ultimately, a blank apathy settled on most of the long-term unemployed, worn down by hunger and idleness. Men drifted on to the streets where they passed the hours seeking a little company and hoping vaguely for some opportunity to turn up. An observer in a Pennsylvania steel town wrote: 'Men stood around listlessly ... half-starved for so long that they had no spirit left.'

Beaten by the Depression

In the autumn of 1930 a mechanic in Houston, Texas, was driven to suicide. He left a note explaining his action:

'This depression has got me licked. There is no work to be had. I can't accept charity and ... I am too honest to steal. So I see no other course. A land flowing with milk and honey and a first-class mechanic can't make an honest living. I would rather take my chances with a just God than with unjust humanity.'
(Quoted in Badger, *The New Deal*)

There was a lot of disorganized anger against the rich and politicians – of the kind that found expression in the Bonus Army protest. A few unemployed, probably about one in 20, expressed anger in action by joining organizations such as the Unemployed Councils that appeared across the USA. They agitated for payment of relief or physically resisted the eviction of people behind with their rent. But, brought up to believe that the USA was the land of opportunity, the American unemployed mostly experienced an overwhelming sense of failure. Sherwood Anderson, an author, observed: 'People seem to blame themselves.'

Chaotic and inadequate welfare provision

There was no nationwide system of unemployment insurance or welfare benefits in the USA. Out of work, people first turned to their family or local community for support. Those who had jobs were expected to share the product of their good fortune with others. Any individuals with an income might find themselves surrounded by dozens of relatives or neighbours expecting handouts. But as work disappeared and unemployment became more or less permanent, inevitably money dried up. Families did what they could to economize. They cut back on food. They took in lodgers, or shared

March 1933: farmers march through St Paul, Minnesota, protesting a lack of government relief funds.

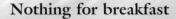

Nothing for breakfast

In his autobiography, an African American writer, Richard Wright, described the humiliating moment when, as an unemployed young man in Chicago in 1930, he was forced to seek food from the city's emergency welfare scheme:

'One morning I rose and my mother told me that there was no food for breakfast. I knew that the city had opened relief stations, but each time I thought of going into one of them I burned with shame. I sat four hours, fighting hunger, avoiding my mother's eyes. Then I rose, put on my hat and coat, and went out ... to plead for bread.'
(Wright, *American Hunger*)

An unemployed apple-seller stands in front of his makeshift home.

cramped housing with another family to halve their rent payments. They sold or pawned their few treasured possessions. Their children went around with holes in their clothes and shoes. As a last resort, the unemployed would enrol for whatever public relief was available, from the city authorities or from charities.

In general, the provision of relief was chaotic and wholly inadequate to cope with permanent mass unemployment. In 1930, for example, about 6,000 of the unemployed in New York City were given surplus apples to sell at 5 cents each. These apple-sellers were one of the sights of Manhattan, but the gesture was not even the beginning of a solution to the problem posed by the workless.

Across the USA, people queued for meals from soup kitchens run by churches or local ethnic organizations. City authorities generally provided either cash or food orders, which could be exchanged for groceries at specified stores. But both cities and charities were soon overstretched by the demands being made on

New York, 1930:
unemployed men queue
for Sunday dinner at the
municipal lodging house.

them. City finances were in any case badly hit by falling tax revenue, which was a natural result of the Depression. By 1932, in many places, public employees such as teachers were no longer being paid because the authorities simply did not have the money for their wages. Similarly, there was no money for relief for the unemployed. Increasingly, payments of cash relief or food orders were liable to be stopped suddenly and without warning, claimants returning home empty-handed.

When even public relief ran out, an unemployed man became, in the words of one Pennsylvanian observer, like 'a stray cat prowling for food'. Some turned to begging. The number of 'panhandlers' was the most visible sign of the crisis on American streets – the song that summed up the Depression for most Americans was 'Buddy, Can You Spare a Dime'. At worst, families were found living off wild dandelions and rotten vegetables salvaged from dustbins. Despite the widespread belief to the contrary, nobody seems to have actually starved, but many may have died of diseases brought on by malnutrition.

Shocking sight

An American woman described a scene she had witnessed in Chicago in 1932:

'One vivid, gruesome moment of those dark days we shall never forget. We saw a crowd of some 50 men fighting over a barrel of garbage, which had been set outside the back door of a restaurant. American citizens fighting for scraps of food like animals!'
(Quoted in Allen, *Since Yesterday*)

Writing home from a hobos' camp, 1938.

Wandering hobos

Teenagers often left home in search of work, 'hitting the road' at the age of 16 or 17 with the encouragement of their families, who saw it as 'one less mouth to feed'. By 1932, an estimated 200,000 Americans, mostly youths or young men, were living as 'hobos'. Penniless vagrants, they hitchhiked on the expanding network of highways or rode the roofs of freight cars on the railroads that criss-crossed the USA. There were sometimes more people riding free on freight trains than on passenger services on the same routes.

Hobos had a hard life. Once on the move, they had little chance to stop. Most towns had regulations that allowed vagrants a one-night stay only. Public relief or some charity might provide a bed and a meal. Then the hobos were shipped out in the morning. Work was almost non-existent. Many hobos resorted at times to minor theft to survive – grabbing a pair of trousers from a clothes-line or

'I was a burden'

One American described how, aged 18, he left home in the summer of 1933 for the life of a wandering hobo:

'It was the Depression; there was no work. I was a burden to Mother and Gus, my stepfather ... [I] told Mother I was leaving. She didn't fight it, but she was sad. Mother owned no suitcase ... All she had was a black satin bag, the size of a pillow case. I jammed my new sleeping bag inside it, three or four pairs of socks, shorts, an old sweater ... Mother made two sandwiches. She went to her purse and gave me all the money she had: 72 cents ... I turned and left, the black satin bag over my shoulder.' (www.pbs.org *Riding the Rails*)

New status

When parents were unemployed, sons frequently became the chief source of family income. This gave them a new independence with regard to their parents, as one teenager pointed out:

'I remind them who makes the money. They don't say much. They just take it, that's all. I'm not the one on relief.'
(Quoted in Degler, *Out of the Past*)

eggs from a hen house. On the trains and in the rail yards, they were harassed by often violent railroad police. Travelling on freight trains was in any case an extremely dangerous activity. The riskiest moment was when a hobo climbed aboard a moving train. One slip could – and often did – lead to a fall under the wheels.

Death fall

Travelling on freight trains as a hobo was a dangerous business. One 17-year-old, roaming around Arizona and California in 1932, made friends with another hobo his own age. But the friendship ended in disaster:

Hobos hazardously board a moving freight train.

'All went well with us, until one night when Jim and I were riding on the ladders between two boxcars. It was so cold my hands nearly froze ... Being back to back, I couldn't see Jim ... All of a sudden the train gave a jerk ... I heard Jim let out a muffled moan, as he fell. I whirled round and made a grab for him. He had on a knit cap. I got the cap and a handful of blond hair. Jim was gone. Disappeared under the wheels.'
(www.pbs.org *Riding the Rails*)

A Hooverville in Seattle, July 1934. There were such shantytowns on the outskirts of most American cities.

The fate that most families feared worst was eviction from their home for failing to pay the mortgage or rent. In 1932 alone, about 250,000 families in American towns and cities suffered this fate. Finding yourself on the street with your few belongings in a handcart could be the beginning of a slippery slope to life in a dreary hostel for the homeless or to a grim existence in one of the shanty towns that sprang up on the edges of American cities – ironically called 'Hoovervilles', after the president whom many Americans blamed for their misfortunes.

Hoover is blamed

The vilification of President Hoover was not altogether fair. He had taken vigorous measures to counter the Depression. He had at first tried to increase demand by putting more money in people's pockets, both by cutting taxes and by persuading industrialists to stop cutting wages. He had invested billions of dollars in construction projects through the Reconstruction Finance Corporation in an effort to create jobs and stimulate the economy. But he had remained adamantly opposed to giving government money directly to the unemployed. And he had eventually given in to the orthodox view that government income and expenditure had to balance, leading to a massive rise in taxes in 1932 and an accompanying sharp reduction in government spending – including wage cuts for government employees.

In the end, Hoover had grappled with the situation as best he could, but had only succeeded in looking heartless and incompetent. By the time of the 1932 presidential election, Depression-struck America was looking for a saviour. They were to find the man they wanted in Hoover's opponent, Franklin D. Roosevelt.

In 1932, an American cartoonist suggested that all the nation's problems would be solved by a 'smilette', a gadget forcing people to 'smile their way back to prosperity'.

Excessive prosperity

Not everyone was hit by the Depression, and as always in such times many prosperous people believed unemployment was the fault of the unemployed. In 1931 a building contractor from Minneapolis wrote a letter to warn President Hoover:

'There is not five per cent of the poverty, distress and general unemployment that many of your enemies would have us believe ... In three cases out of four, the unemployed is looking for a very light job at very heavy pay, and with the privilege of being provided with an automobile if he is required to walk more than four or five blocks a day.'
(Quoted in McElvaine, *Down and Out in the Great Depression*)

WORLD CRISIS

The onset of the Great Depression in the early 1930s was most striking in the USA, where it contrasted starkly with the confidence and optimism of the 1920s boom. But the shock waves of economic crisis reverberated across the entire world.

This was partly a direct consequence of events in the USA. The withdrawal of US investment hit Europe – especially Germany – and South America very hard indeed. So did the drying up of the US market for imported goods. When the American motor industry suddenly cut back on production of automobiles, for example, demand for rubber for tyres slumped, ruining the owners of rubber plantations in Malaya and destroying the livelihood of the local people who worked

Workers in Chile's nitrate industry, distant victims of the downturn in North American farming.

Long-distance effect

Hundreds of thousands of people in Chile, South America, lived by producing nitrates that were sold to North American farmers for use as fertilizer. When farming in Canada and the USA collapsed in the Depression, the impact on Chilean workers was swift and devastating. One woman later described the sense of shock and hopelessness:

'It was our bread, our bread was the nitrate. That was our security and that was our life. We didn't have anything else. One day in December we knew that they were closing the works. They did not come to talk to the people. They just gave the orders ... We were left with nothing. What could we do?' (Quoted in Hodgson, *People's Century*)

for them. When belt-tightening Americans drank less coffee, workers on Brazilian coffee plantations were laid off and went hungry. Falling demand for luxury silk goods in the shops of Manhattan meant poverty and unemployment for employees of silk factories in Japan.

The wider world also fell victim to some of the same problems that had undermined American prosperity. Just as in the USA, a key factor in the global economy was agricultural overproduction. Farmers in Canada were producing more wheat than they could sell; sheep farmers in Australia were producing too much wool. As prices on the world market plummeted, these 'primary producers' no longer had the money to buy the manufactured goods that they traditionally imported from the industrialized countries of western Europe. So, again, a vicious downward spiral set in. As the exports of the industrialized countries went into decline, they had less money to spend on imports. So demand for products such as wheat and wool fell, further lowering prices, which in turn further depressed demand for industrial exports, and so on.

An unemployed worker at the London docks.

The collapse of world trade

The collapse of world trade was as spectacular in its way as the collapse of American industry and agriculture. Between 1929 and 1933, trade shrank by 60 per cent. That is, for every five merchant ships that had made trading voyages in 1929, only two plied the seas four years later. Apart from anything else, this decline obviously had a devastating effect on the livelihood of dockworkers, shipbuilders and merchant seamen.

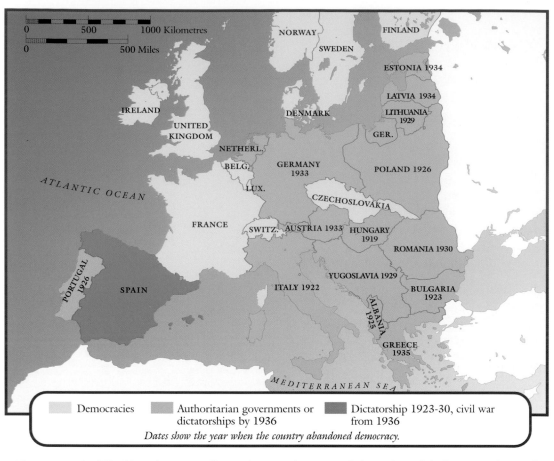

Democracies	Authoritarian governments or dictatorships by 1936	Dictatorship 1923-30, civil war from 1936

Dates show the year when the country abandoned democracy.

The economic difficulties of the 1920s and 1930s in Europe were reflected in a sharp turn away from democratic government. Spain bucked the trend in 1930 with a revolution that replaced a dictatorship with a democratic republic, but in 1936 civil war broke out and right-wing dictator General Francisco Franco took power in 1939.

Countries mostly responded to the crisis in ways that only made it worse. Governments cut spending in an effort to keep their finances stable. Instead of co-operating to boost trade, they introduced 'protectionist' measures to defend their own agriculture and industries against imports from abroad. The USA set the example for this in 1930 with the Smoot-Hawley tariff, which imposed a heavy duty on agricultural imports. These selfish 'beggar-my-neighbour' policies mostly worked to the general disadvantage. As everyone took steps to block everyone else's exports, hardly anyone was able to trade effectively.

Between 1929 and 1932, the output of Europe's factories fell drastically – by about a third, for example, in Italy and France. In most parts of Europe, unemployment rose sharply. In Britain, over 2 million people were out of work in 1930 and almost 3 million in 1931. In Germany, the situation was much worse. Unemployment there already stood at 3 million by

1929 and two years later it had risen to over 5 million. According to some unofficial estimates, almost one-half of Germans were either unemployed or on short-time working by the end of 1932.

The European welfare system

Europe's unemployed were, on the whole, much better provided for than their American counterparts, because many European countries had some kind of welfare system for those out of work and for the needy in general. Britain was not untypical. The dole – unemployment insurance – had first been provided for most British industrial workers in the early 1920s. The unemployed had to make regular visits to the labour exchange to 'sign on', proving they were 'available for work', even though jobs mostly just did not exist. Regulations varied, but some unemployed workers had to sign on every day, and, in the case of dockers, even twice a day. As long as they signed on, they had a right to a regular payment that amounted to about half the national average wage.

After a fixed period, the long-term unemployed were shifted on to public assistance, a form of benefit which depended on officials estimating the needs of them and their family. If they

Unemployed cotton workers outside the labour exchange in Oldham, May 1931.

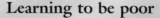

Learning to be poor

When a middle-class Liverpool man went bankrupt in the Depression, people had to explain to him how to survive in poverty. His daughter described what he learned:

'There were agencies in the town, he was told, which would provide the odd pair of shoes or an old blanket for a child ... An open fire, he was assured, could be kept going all day from the refuse of the streets, old shoes, scraps of paper, twigs, wooden boxes, potato peelings ... Pawnbrokers would take almost anything saleable, and one could buy second-hand clothing from them ... '
(Quoted in Stevenson, *British Society 1914-45*)

reckoned that the family was not sufficiently hard up – perhaps because they had some savings or had a grandparent living with them who was drawing a pension – the officials would cut benefit payments. This 'means test' was a humiliating experience for the unemployed and one of the bitterest causes of resentment in Britain in the 1930s.

The dole and public assistance guaranteed most British people against absolute poverty. A sense of despair hung over the

The town that died

Author J. B. Priestley visited the shipbuilding town of Jarrow on the Tyne, a notorious unemployment black spot after its shipyard closed in 1933. He described the scene on the streets:

'One out of every two shops appeared to be permanently closed. Wherever we went there were men hanging about, not scores of them but hundreds and thousands of them ... The men wore the drawn masks of prisoners of war.'
(Priestley, *English Journey*)

devastated communities of Tyneside or South Wales, where the closed works or slag-heap often dominated the town. In these places, author J. B. Priestley wrote, 'nothing, it seemed, would ever happen again'. But because living standards in general had risen in Britain, an unemployed person in the 1930s was likely to be no worse off than his father had been when in work 20 years earlier. Similarly, in Germany poverty in the Depression was not as extreme as it had been a decade earlier, in the chaotic aftermath of the First World War.

Political repercussions

Unemployment benefits, however, did little to lessen the psychological and political impact of the Depression in Europe. There was an especially dramatic crisis in the summer of 1931, when the Kreditanstalt bank in Austria collapsed, dragging down two of Germany's largest banks with it. The German government reacted to this financial crisis by cutting spending and raising taxes – measures certain to worsen the country's already shocking unemployment figures. There was a serious threat that the financial storm sweeping Germany would also engulf the City of London. Under pressure from

A crowd outside a bank in Berlin, after its failure in July 1931.

financiers and bankers, the British government cut unemployment benefits and the wages of government employees, including sailors in the Royal Navy. These cuts provoked hostile demonstrations, including a brief mutiny in the fleet at Invergordon. As confidence in the economy plummeted, in September 1931 Britain was forced to abandon the 'gold standard', which had underpinned the value of the pound. Sterling rapidly lost about a quarter of its value on foreign exchanges.

The 1931 crisis brought down a recently elected Labour government in Britain. It was replaced by a coalition National Government, soon dominated by the Conservatives. This was a mild political upset compared with that experienced by many countries. Throughout the world, governments were overthrown as national economies slumped. In Latin America, 12 countries changed their governments in two years, 10 of them as a result of military coups. In India, West Africa, Indonesia and the West Indies, political movements opposed to rule by European colonialists gathered fresh strength. In Germany, voters desperate for a solution to the economic crisis

Angry protest

When the British government cut unemployment benefit in 1931, there were angry demonstrations. Some, as in Salford, Greater Manchester, ended in violence. Writer Walter Greenwood described the start of the protest:

'The long room where the men drew their dole [was] crowded, the voices of the men loud, harsh and angry, a volume of sound that intensified and increased as latecomers, having their money pushed to them with 10 per cent deducted, glared at the cashiers and denounced them angrily ... Under the direction of a few organizers the crowd's formlessness was urged into ranks in the middle of the roadway ... A large red flag was unfurled at the procession's head. A big drum materialized from nowhere, it seemed, and to its hollow and rhythmic beat, the march began towards the main road and the Town Hall.' (Greenwood, *There Was A Time*)

The new military rulers of Peru, Colonel Luis M. Sanchez Cerro (centre) and his cabinet, after a coup in September 1930. Most countries in Latin America experienced political upheavals as the depression ruined their economies.

increasingly backed extremist parties, especially the Communists and Adolf Hitler's National Socialists (Nazis). In Spain, a revolution in 1931 created a left-wing republic.

In Scandinavia, too, mass unemployment led to intense social conflict. In 1931 some workers in Sweden went on strike in protest at wage cuts in the wood pulp and paper industries. The army was called in and five people were shot dead at the town of Adalen. The public outcry provoked by this event brought a sweeping election victory for Sweden's radical Social Democrat Party.

Naturally, people puzzled over what was happening to the world economy. Conventional economists argued that the Depression was simply a severe example of a normal downturn in the cycle of business and trade. In this view, all governments had to do was keep their budgets balanced and wait for the economic upswing that would inevitably follow. But as the Depression deepened, this attitude commanded less and less support.

'We are for Adolf Hitler' said the workers in this Nazi Party poster in 1933.

The Soviet model

Soviet dictator Joseph Stalin was admired by many people in the West, who thought his communist policies held the answer to the Depression.

An alternative view was available that seemed to make perfect sense of what was happening. Marxist communist revolutionaries had always argued that capitalism – the existing world system of business and finance – was a rotten structure that would one day go into terminal crisis and collapse. With the Depression, it seemed to many people that the bankruptcy of the capitalist system was self-evident. There was a surge of interest in, and admiration for, the communist Soviet Union. Just as the Depression struck, Soviet dictator Joseph Stalin had embarked on a massive industrialization drive in the first Five-Year Plan (1929-33). As factories in the USA and western Europe closed their doors, in the Soviet Union new factories were being built.

Distant admirers who saw the Soviet Union as the only country to have bucked the Depression were far from understanding the reality of Soviet life. In the early 1930s, millions of Soviet citizens died of famine. Millions more worked as slave labourers after being carried off as prisoners to the camps of the Soviet 'Gulag'. Even free workers in the Soviet Union led incredibly hard lives, labouring for long hours in harsh conditions for appallingly low wages.

Admiring Russia

During the Depression, many Americans saw communist Russia as, at least in some ways, an example worth imitating. Will Rogers, one of the most popular comedians in the USA in the 1930s, expressed this view with a wry comment on unemployment:

'Those rascals in Russia, along with their cuckoo stuff, have got some mighty good ideas ... Just think of everybody in a country going to work!'
(Quoted in Johnson, *A History of the Modern World*)

Soviet reality

In 1932-33, a terrible famine gripped Ukraine, then part of the Soviet Union. It was largely caused by the Soviet authorities seizing all available grain from the peasants. A Communist Party official later remembered the scene in one Ukrainian city:

'Dniepropetrovsk was overrun with starving peasants. Many of them lay listless, too weak even to beg around the railway stations. Their children were little more than skeletons with swollen bellies.'
(Quoted in Mazower, *Dark Continent*)

Yet, psychologically, admiration for the Soviet system was perhaps understandable. One Soviet citizen later remembered the 1930s as a time when, for all the hardships, many people in the Soviet Union 'lived with hope of a radiant future'. It was precisely the ability to inspire hope for the future that was so totally lacking in the governments of North America and western Europe – at least until 1933, when major changes came over the political landscape.

Young apprentices at a factory in the Soviet-ruled Ukraine. No one was allowed to photograph the famine that killed millions of Ukrainians in 1932-33.

NEW DEALS

In November 1932, the USA held its first presidential election since the Great Depression had started. The Republicans put up President Hoover as their candidate. Not surprisingly, given the state of the American economy, he was soundly defeated by the Democratic Party candidate, Franklin D. Roosevelt.

A wealthy landowner, Roosevelt had fought back after a crippling attack of polio in 1921, which had threatened to end his political career. As governor of New York since 1928, he had won respect for his efforts to provide relief for the unemployed. During the campaign for the presidency, Roosevelt promised the American people a 'New Deal' and expressed his concern for 'the forgotten man at the bottom of the economic pyramid'. But what exactly he intended to do to solve the economic crisis was left vague.

4 March 1933: newly inaugurated president Franklin D. Roosevelt (centre) arrives at the White House with his wife Eleanor and their son, James.

Roosevelt became president at a moment of acute financial crisis. Since October 1932, state after state had declared 'bank holidays', closing their banks to prevent a run on funds, as the failure of some banks led to panic withdrawals from others. Roosevelt took instant dramatic action to restore confidence. He declared a nationwide bank holiday, closing every bank in the USA from 6 March 1933. A law, passed in three days, declared that banks would only be allowed to reopen after the federal authorities had established that they were reliable.

Listening to the radio. Roosevelt made regular radio broadcasts to the American people.

Then, in his first radio broadcast as president, Roosevelt assured Americans that their money was now safer in banks than in their mattresses. It worked. During the following month most banks reopened, and customers stepped forward to deposit their money. Other legislation followed to strengthen the banking system, as well as outlawing many of the bad practices on the stock exchange that had contributed to the Great Crash.

'The only thing we have to fear ... '

Roosevelt's inauguration speech, on 4 March 1933, was a dramatic call for bold measures to conquer the Depression. It struck a chord with Americans sure their country was drifting onto the rocks. Roosevelt said:

'So, first of all, let me assert my firm belief that the only thing we have to fear is fear itself – nameless, unreasoning, unjustified terror which paralyses needed efforts to convert retreat into advance ... The people of the United States have not failed. In their need they have registered a mandate that they want direct, vigorous action.'

The cover of the music for a 1933 song celebrating the National Recovery Administration, a centre-piece of the New Deal.

The New Deal

In his first hundred days as president, Roosevelt pushed through a large and varied programme of legislation that laid the foundations of his New Deal. He was an experimenter rather than a clear logical thinker, and many of his measures were contradictory. For example, one of his first actions was to cut wages for federal employees, even the lowest paid, and reduce pensions for war veterans. Yet other parts of the New Deal programme were designed to raise wages and prices, since Roosevelt's advisers had told him that higher wages and higher prices would stimulate industry and agriculture, and get the country working again.

The Agricultural Adjustment Act was aimed at raising farm prices. Farmers were in effect to be paid by the government to cut their output. Soon, controversially, land was being left fallow and piglets were being slaughtered, even though some Americans were near to starvation. Meanwhile, the National Recovery Administration (NRA), set up under General Hugh Johnson,

Paid in cash

Most of the unemployed taken on to New Deal schemes were delighted to be no longer dependent on relief hand-outs, even if the pay for their work was low. One Chicago man, given work by the Civil Works Administration (CWA), described how he had hated food relief orders, or 'tickets':

'I hated going to the store with a ticket. Everybody would look at you. Everyone knew you were on relief right away. On CWA there were no tickets to go to the grocery store any more. My mother bought for cash.' (Quoted in Badger, *The New Deal*)

pressured businesses into following guidelines on wages and prices, with the aim of increasing demand and making it profitable to reopen factories. The NRA's nationwide propaganda effort was one of the most visible signs of the New Deal, as businesses across the land sported the NRA logo to show their commitment to supporting the government's recovery programme.

Roosevelt's most popular innovations were immediate measures to tackle poverty and unemployment. The Federal Emergency Relief Administration was entrusted with $500 million to hand out to states to subsidize their relief programmes for the unemployed. More importantly, government organizations – first the Civil Works Administration (CWA) and later the Works Progress Administration (WPA) – were set up to tackle unemployment head on. Hundreds of thousands of unemployed Americans were enrolled on government work schemes. These ranged, over the years, from major construction projects to 'boondoggles' – futile jobs that were invented simply to

The Civil Works Administration put thousands of unemployed Americans to work on construction projects and other government schemes.

Some of the earliest recruits to the Civilian Conservation Corps in California in 1933. American youths found service with the CCC a rewarding alternative to unemployment.

provide work. The Civilian Conservation Corps (CCC), which enrolled unemployed youths, was dedicated almost entirely to tree planting in a valiant attempt to reverse soil erosion across the USA. There were later even employment schemes for unemployed writers, actors, musicians and artists, who covered thousands of American public buildings with decorative murals.

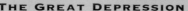

Hard work and square meals

One American remembered how he joined the Civilian Conservation Corps, a New Deal youth employment scheme, in the 1930s:

'My mother who was trying to raise my six older bothers and sisters, couldn't afford another mouth to feed. So I enlisted in the Civilian Conservation Corps ... These big trees you see along the highways – all these big forests was all built by the CCC ... We just dug trenches and kept planting trees. You could plant about a hundred an hour. I really enjoyed it. I had three wonderful square meals a day. No matter what they put on the table, we ate and were glad to get it ... '
(Quoted in Terkel, *Hard Times*)

Voice of hope

A doctor from Chicago remembered the impact of Roosevelt, especially his ability to connect with ordinary people through radio broadcasts:

'It was the hopeful voice of FDR that got this thing out of the swamps. He didn't have much to offer, but it was enough. He was a guy flexible enough to understand the need for experiments, for not being rigid, and for making people feel there was somebody who gave a damn about them.'
(Quoted in Terkel, *Hard Times*)

Another New Deal initiative was the setting up of the Tennessee Valley Authority (TVA). The role of the TVA was to develop the economy of a whole region of the impoverished, backward rural South. Dams were built to supply the region with electricity for the first time and to provide irrigation for agriculture. Earnest young New Dealers flocked to the Tennessee Valley to show the local hillbillies how to use electrical appliances in their shacks and farmsteads.

In the 1930s many new dams were built to provide electricity to rural America.

Roosevelt raises morale

The exact impact of the New Deal on the US economy is much disputed. Certainly, from 1933 to 1937 production increased and the number of jobless fell. Yet mass unemployment remained a fact of American life, with about one in eight people still out of work. Roosevelt's impact on the morale of the nation was, however, unquestionable. Millions of people felt that they had hope again – and that they owed this to the president.

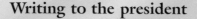

Writing to the president

Thousands of Americans wrote letters to President and Mrs Roosevelt, convinced that they would intervene personally to help with their problems. In 1936, one child from Chicago wrote:

'Dear Mr President: I'm a boy of 12 years old. I want to tell you about my family. My father hasn't worked for five months. He went plenty times to relief, he filled out application. They won't give us anything. Please do something ... All the time [my father's] crying because he can't find work. I told him why are you crying daddy, and daddy said why shouldn't I cry when there is nothing in the house. I feel sorry for him. That night I couldn't sleep. The next morning I wrote this letter to you.'
(Quoted in McElvaine, *Down and Out in the Great Depression*)

Roosevelt won the hearts of ordinary Americans. In his regular radio broadcasts – presented as 'fireside chats' – he made his listeners feel that he was on their side. He addressed them as 'my friends', and most believed he meant it. He invited them to 'tell me your troubles', and they did, writing to the White House in their thousands. His popularity soared. When journalist Martha Gellhorn toured parts of the USA in 1934, she reported: 'Every house I visited – millworker or unemployed – had a picture of the president.'

Still, the New Deal was certainly not universally popular. Some people were disappointed that it was not more radical and did not challenge the capitalist system. Left-wing critics argued that agricultural subsidies mostly benefited big landowners and that NRA price-fixing favoured big business. But the fiercest criticism of Roosevelt came from rich conservatives. They denounced the interference of federal government in all aspects of economic life and derided Roosevelt as an enemy of free enterprise. The conservative Supreme Court became locked in conflict with the president, ruling that major New Deal measures, including the NRA, were unconstitutional.

Instead of being cowed by the rich and the newspapers they controlled, in 1935 Roosevelt shifted his administration in a more radical direction. In what is sometimes called the Second New Deal, a Social Security Act established schemes for unemployment benefit and old age pensions which, although very limited, at least gave the USA the beginnings of a social welfare system. Also, the Wagner Act introduced new rules on relations between workers and their employers, effectively giving labour unions far more rights than they had ever enjoyed before in the USA.

In 1936, a presidential election gave the American people their chance to show what they really thought of the New Deal. It was a triumph for Roosevelt. Ignoring savage campaigns against the president in the press, Americans re-elected him to the White House by a landslide. Roosevelt won over 27 million votes compared with his opponent's 16 million.

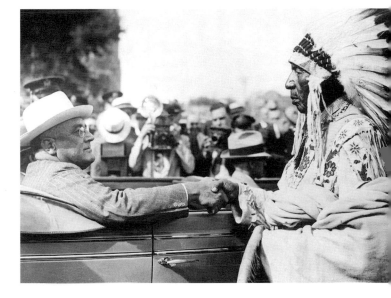

Roosevelt meets a Sioux Indian chief, 1936. Minorities such as Native Americans benefited from the New Deal.

Hated by the rich

Roosevelt was as hated by the rich as he was loved by the poor. Crossing the Atlantic on an ocean liner in the 1930s, American writer Thomas Wolfe happened to mention that he supported the president. He described the outraged reaction of his wealthy American fellow-passengers:

'I was told that if I voted for this vile Communist, this sinister fascist, this scheming and contriving socialist and his gang of conspirators, I had no longer any right to consider myself an American citizen.'
(Quoted in Johnson, *A History of the Modern World*)

Hitler takes power in Germany

Roosevelt was not the only leader offering a new deal to his Depression-hit people. Nazi leader Adolf Hitler's rise to power in Germany occurred at almost exactly the same time as Roosevelt's in the USA. Hitler had no interest in economics. His solution to high unemployment and industrial decline was to unite the German people behind a powerful leader – himself – ending the divisions brought about by democracy. Strong and united, Germany would overcome the enemies whom Hitler deemed responsible for all the German people's sufferings, especially the Jews.

23 October 1933: Adolf Hitler shovels a spade of earth to launch the building of a new motorway. A programme of road-building was one of the measures introduced to lift Germany out of depression.

Hitler's view of the world was a paranoid delusion, but his rise to power was nonetheless followed by the rapid disappearance of mass unemployment. The reasons for this were mixed. It was partly just one example of a general economic recovery that was seen in many countries from 1933. It was also partly the result of massive government spending, especially on arms production, as Hitler sought to make Germany a great military power once more. Work-creation schemes were backed up by compulsory labour service – long-term unemployment was in effect turned into a punishable crime. Jobs were also created for men by forcing women out of paid work, since the Nazis considered that a woman's place was in the home.

Conquering unemployment was one of the keys to Hitler's immense popularity in Germany in the mid-1930s. Even the Nazis' bitterest enemies found it hard to argue against. Hitler's example gave encouragement to extreme right-wing fascist movements in other countries, including Sir Oswald Mosley's British Union of Fascists. In common with communist admirers of the Soviet Union, admirers of the Nazis argued that the system of 'liberal capitalism', based on free enterprise, individual freedom and free trade, had been proved bankrupt by the

Depression. The future, fascists argued, lay with strong corporate states aggressively promoting their national economies under strict direction and control.

In reality, the German recovery was not as impressive as it seemed. By 1937, economic problems were building up once more. The Nazis' answer was first to plunder the assets of Jewish citizens, seizing their money and businesses, and then to embark on military expansion and conquest.

Cheering admirers of Hitler in 1935: the ending of unemployment under Nazi rule contributed to Hitler's popularity in Germany.

Scandinavia finds another solution

A more durable and humane response to the Depression was found in Scandinavia. Sweden, in particular, recovered dramatically in the 1930s under governments dominated by Social Democrats. They abandoned the traditional concern for balancing government income and expenditure. Instead, they deliberately boosted the economy by running a budget deficit. Much of the money was spent on beginning to establish a true welfare state, in which the government would effectively take responsibility for looking after the health and well-being of its people from the cradle to the grave. Between 1932 and 1937, Sweden's economy expanded rapidly and unemployment shrank to an acceptable level. One foreign observer referred to Swedish democratic socialism as 'the most encouraging thing in the world today'.

Roosevelt was not a socialist or a fascist. He wanted to be seen as the man who had saved American capitalism and American democracy. He could not bring himself to reject the traditional belief in a balanced budget and constraint on government spending. After his great 1936 election victory he cut spending, believing that free enterprise was now healthy enough to return to the helm. The result was an immediate steep rise in unemployment, which came close to pre-New Deal levels in 1937. Despite the best efforts of their rulers, for many Americans and millions of other people in countries across the world, the Depression seemed a fact of life that would never go away.

LIVING WITH THE DEPRESSION

In the 1930s movie *The Wizard of Oz*, Dorothy, played by Judy Garland, is transported from Depression-struck America to a magical land of fantasy – mirroring the effect the movies had on the cinema-going public.

In its most comprehensive form, the Great Depression lasted from 1929 to 1933. From that date there was a general recovery, not only in countries such as the USA and Nazi Germany, where dramatic government action was taken, but also in Britain, where the government response was conservative and low-key. Britain was one of many countries in which economic output reached and surpassed its 1929 level during the second half of the 1930s.

Progress and modernization

In some ways, the 1930s were years of notable progress and modernization. In Europe and North America, millions of homes were supplied with electricity for the first time. Workers who had jobs found that their wages stretched to many small luxuries as prices stayed low. Millions of people went to the movies more than once a week and to a dancehall on a Saturday night. Crowds at sports events were huge, and the popularity of healthy leisure activities such as hiking and swimming boomed. In many European countries, including Britain and France, working people got paid holidays for the first time. Standards of healthcare and housing improved. In Britain, the 1930s were notable for the number of council houses built to rehouse people from insanitary slums.

Fun for kids

An old man interviewed in the USA in 1938 was struck by how much life for the young had improved despite the Depression:

'The kids today don't realize how much variety they've got to pick from for amusement. When I was a youngster we didn't have much. There wasn't even many books. Now they got books and radios and moving pictures and toy autos and airplanes and scooters and God knows what all.' (Interview, Federal Writers' Project, Library of Congress)

But in other ways the Depression did not go away. During the 1930s, world trade failed to recover to its 1929 level. Most countries pursued greater self-sufficiency, defending their industries and agriculture against imports and trying to produce more for their own home markets, rather than for export. Neither money nor goods could be moved freely across borders. Where trade existed, it was conducted largely under the terms of special deals between governments. Under the system of 'imperial preference', for example, Britain traded mostly with the countries of its empire and commonwealth. Germany had special trade agreements with the countries of south-eastern Europe.

Rural America suffered

Within countries, economic recovery bypassed some parts of the population, which remained in apparently permanent poverty. Much of rural America, in particular, remained in Depression throughout the 1930s. Probably the poorest people in the USA were blacks in the rural South. They were untouched by the efforts of the New Deal and continued to migrate

Nothing new

Long accustomed to poverty, an African-American from a rural area of Georgia in the Deep South commented wryly:

'Most blacks did not even know the Great Depression had come. They had always been poor and only thought the whites were catching up.' (Quoted in Badger, *The New Deal*)

1937: blacks queuing for government relief disprove the claim of the poster behind them.

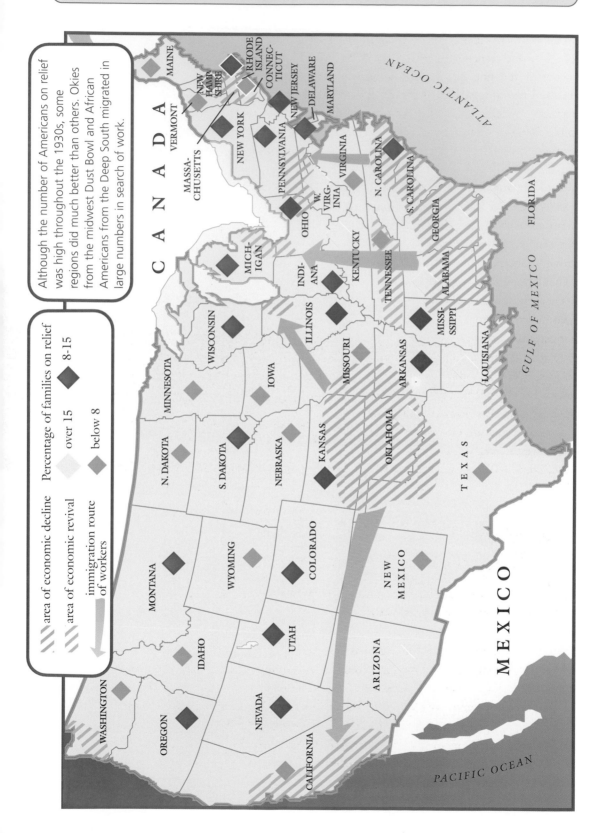

Although the number of Americans on relief was high throughout the 1930s, some regions did much better than others. Okies from the midwest Dust Bowl and African Americans from the Deep South migrated in large numbers in search of work.

area of economic decline

area of economic revival

immigration route of workers

Percentage of families on relief

over 15

8-15

below 8

to the northern cities in their hundreds of thousands in search of a new life. Tenant farmers – those who farmed a piece of land they did not own – generally had a hard time in the 1930s. They were driven off the land in great numbers, as the introduction of tractors and other machinery made it more profitable for landowners to create large farms that they could exploit themselves.

Most dramatic was the fate of the farmers of the Great Plains. Bad farming practices prepared the way for an ecological disaster when drought struck the region in 1933. When winds were high, dry topsoil blew away, forming vast dust storms that destroyed crops and half-buried farmsteads across vast areas of the Midwest. With their livelihood gone, at least 500,000 of the 'Okies' – so called because many of them came from Oklahoma – loaded their few possessions on an old jalopy and drove west to seek work on the farms of California. There, life was almost

South Dakota, May 1936: dust and sand have covered a car and farm machinery.

Shattered dreams

A wheat farmer from Kansas described the devastating impact of the dust storms of the 1930s:

'With the gales came the dust. Sometimes it was so thick that it completely hid the sun. Visibility ranged from nothing to 50 feet, the former when the eyes were filled with dirt which could not be avoided, even with goggles ... When I knew that my crop was irrevocably gone, I experienced a deathly feeling which I hope can affect a man only once in a lifetime. My dreams and ambitions had been flouted by nature and my shattered ideals seemed gone for ever.'
(Quoted in Svobida, *Farming the Dustbowl*)

July 1938: Arthur Rothstein sets up his camera on a hill overlooking Aliquippa, Pennsylvania, in order to take photographs of the steel mills for the FSA.

Photographed for the FSA in St Mary's County, Maryland: the daughter of a family who received FSA aid in 1940 to cultivate a vegetable garden.

as tough as back in the Dust Bowl. Living in makeshift camps, the migrants earned rock-bottom wages for temporary work, and suffered brutal harassment if they ever dared protest about pay or conditions.

In 1937, the Farm Security Administration (FSA) was set up, a late-coming New Deal organization that was intended to concentrate on the needs of the rural poor. It had some effect: for example, providing better accommodation for the 'Okie' migrants in California. But its most famous action was to pay photographers to take photos of the rural poor, producing wonderful pictures that have become the most well-known images of the Depression years.

Industrial communities in Britain suffered

In Britain, although new factories opened in southern England and the midlands making aircraft, cars or electrical goods, the old industrial areas of northern England, Scotland, Northern Ireland and South Wales were ravaged by long-term unemployment. In the worst-hit areas – such as Merthyr in South Wales and Jarrow on the Tyne – the majority of the population was out of work throughout the 1930s. Towns like these had been built around a single industry such as coalmining or shipbuilding. When the mine or shipyard closed down, there simply was no work.

Children in the country

Poverty was also a fact of life in the British countryside in the 1930s. Writer Valentine Ackland described children who had to walk more than two miles to school in all weathers:

'I have seen the children pass, wet and shivering with cold ... boots squelching mud, thin coats dripping ... It is no joke for the mother either, to have five or six half-drowned children returned to her at the end of the day; on the present wages it is not probable that a cottage household owns a complete change of all clothing for each child – even boots and socks are hard enough to find.'
(Quoted in Wright, *The Village that Died for England*)

The workers there had lived all their lives in the same tight-knit community. An unemployed miner probably sang in his local choir. He shopped at his local co-op store and had mates in the local pub. When unemployment struck, many of the younger men moved to southern England or the midlands where jobs were obtainable. But most of the older men were not prepared to move. They stayed in the community they knew and faced a bleak future of permanent unemployment.

Nothing to do, nothing to spend

British working-class writer Walter Greenwood was unemployed as a young man in the Depression. He described the experience:

'You fell into the habit of slouching, of putting your hands into your pockets and keeping them there; of glancing at people, furtively, ashamed of your secret, until you fancied that everybody eyed you with suspicion ... Nothing to do with time; nothing to spend; nothing to do tomorrow nor the day after; nothing to wear; can't get married. A living corpse ... '
(Greenwood, *Love on the Dole*)

Outside toilets and bed bugs

Writer George Orwell travelled through the depressed areas of industrial Britain in 1936-37. In his notebooks he described the terrible conditions in which many people lived; for example, a house in Barnsley, Yorkshire:

'Distance to lavatory 70 yards. Four beds in house for eight people … Parents have one bed, eldest son another, and remaining five people share the other two. Bugs very bad – "You can't keep 'em down when it's 'ot". Indescribable squalor in downstairs room and smell upstairs almost unbearable.'
(Orwell, *The Road to Wigan Pier*)

Long-term unemployment inevitably led to a gradual decline in a family's standard of living. The unemployed ate poorly, with a diet mostly consisting of white bread, potatoes, margarine, jam and tea. Wives and mothers suffered most. According to the Pilgrim Trust, a charity, women were 'literally starving themselves in order to feed and clothe the children reasonably well'. Children often helped the family survive by foraging for coal or doing casual work, such as paper rounds.

New England

At the end of the trip around England that became the subject of his 1934 book *English Journey*, J. B. Priestley wrote about the newly prosperous Britain he had found, away from the old industrial areas where unemployment and poverty prevailed:

'This is the England of arterial and bypass roads, of filling stations and factories that look like exhibition buildings, of giant cinemas and dance-halls and cafes, bungalows with tiny garages, cocktail bars, Woolworth's, motor-coaches, wireless, hiking, factory girls looking like actresses, greyhound racing and dirt tracks, swimming pools … '
(Priestley, *English Journey*)

Social conflict

The fate of the unemployed was easily ignored by the majority of the British population, which was doing very nicely. The National Unemployed Workers Movement, a communist-led group, organized 'hunger marches' to draw attention to the fate of the unemployed. Bodies of jobless men tramped from their industrial towns across the country to London, where their arrival was sometimes the occasion for violent confrontations with the police. The most famous protest against unemployment was the Jarrow March of 1936. Unlike the hunger marches, it was not organized by communists and therefore received a far more favourable press. But it was no more effective in persuading the government to do anything about the unemployment blackspots.

Jarrow marchers on the way to London to hand in their petition, 1936.

Jarrow marchers

In the summer of 1936, 200 unemployed men, handpicked by the local council, marched from the Tyneside town of Jarrow to London to deliver a petition to parliament. A man from Jarrow who had moved to London in search of work witnessed the arrival of the marchers:

'These were lads that I'd spent spare time with and been alongside for years, and I'd seen them slowly disintegrating, a wasted lifetime of standing around ... So you'll appreciate that when I saw them come into Hyde Park, this was something.'
(BBC radio interview)

The level of social conflict in Britain was mild compared with many other countries in the 1930s. In France, a left-wing Popular Front government, including socialists and communists, came to power as a wave of strikes paralysed French industry in 1936. In Spain, in the same year, the election of a Popular Front government was the occasion for army officers to launch an uprising that developed into a prolonged civil war.

Sit-in strikers at a department store entertain themselves during their occupation of their workplace.

In the USA, with labour union membership encouraged by New Deal legislation, a rash of 'sit-in' strikes broke out in the winter of 1936-37. Having downed tools, workers occupied their workplace day and night to prevent strike breakers being brought in to do their jobs. Although all kinds of workplaces became involved, including even restaurants and theatres, the main confrontations were in the automobile and steel industries. A strike involving more than 100,000 workers at 60 General Motors factories won its objectives, but a steel strike was broken up with great violence. In one incident, police attacked strikers outside a factory in Chicago, killing 10 and injuring 90 others, many shot down while attempting to flee.

After the defeat of the steel strike in 1937, the sit-in movement in the USA faded. Roosevelt's New Deal had run out of steam, encountering increasing conservative opposition in the late 1930s. France's reforming Popular Front government fell in 1937, and in Spain right-wing forces won the civil war in 1939. In Britain, the Conservative Party had a secure hold on power throughout the 1930s, easily holding off the challenge of the Labour Party. In the absence of more radical initiatives, there seemed no reason why mass unemployment and the other ills left in the wake of the Great Depression should ever end. But there was a solution, and it arrived in 1939: another world war.

LESSONS LEARNED?

The Depression was one of the major causes of the Second World War. The economic crisis helped bring aggressive militaristic governments to power in Germany and Japan, and it made these governments believe that conquest was the only path to future prosperity and economic security. But it was the outbreak of the Second World War that finally ended the Depression. In Britain, unemployment soon disappeared as over 1 million men were enrolled in the armed forces and industry geared up for war production. Labour shortages became the norm and hundreds of thousands of women took the place of men in factories and working on the land.

Well before the USA entered the war, at the end of 1941, the US economy was booming again. Roosevelt made his country the 'arsenal of democracy', providing arms for Britain to fight with, and in the process creating jobs for Americans in the war

A recruiting sergeant speaks to volunteers, London, 1940. Below: bombers on the assembly line at an aircraft factory in California, 1942.

Safe in the army

In the USA, a former hobo who had spent the 1930s roaming the country on freight trains, recalled:

'When the war came, I was so glad when I got in the army. I knew I was safe. I put a uniform on, and I said, 'Now I'm safe'. I had money comin', I had food comin' ... In the army ... I wasn't gonna starve.'
(Quoted in Terkel, *Hard Times*)

industries. As the war went on, the demand for labour in the USA became so intense that wages rose sharply. Not only women found themselves employed in well-paid factory jobs. African Americans, formerly excluded from the best jobs, found work in war production that gave many an unprecedented taste of prosperity.

Post-war reconstruction

In the course of the war, the leaders of the Western allies – chiefly the USA and Britain – turned their thoughts to post-war reconstruction. There was general agreement that there must be no return to the conditions of the Depression, especially mass unemployment. The views of a British economist, John Maynard Keynes, became highly influential. He had argued in the 1930s that governments could successfully intervene in the economy to guarantee full employment, as long as they would set aside their obsession with balancing budgets and cutting spending. The right to work was enshrined in the charter of the United Nations Organization, set up in 1944. A conference held at Bretton Woods, New Hampshire, in the same year tried to establish a framework for a revival of world trade and international finance after the war.

The disease of unemployment

During the war, even most conservative thinkers came to accept that full employment was a necessary goal of public policy. *The Times*, the newspaper of the British establishment, stated in 1943:

'Next to war, unemployment has been the most widespread, the most insidious, and the most corroding malady of our generation: it is the specific social disease of Western civilization in our time.'
(Quoted in Hobsbawm, *Age of Extremes*)

For almost 30 years after the war, economic performance seemed to offer a remarkable example of lessons having been learned. There was no return to mass unemployment. Rapid economic growth in the USA, Western Europe and Japan brought jobs and rising incomes. World trade flourished. In Western Europe, most countries espoused some version of Keynesian economics and a welfare state, taking responsibility for looking after their citizens in sickness, poverty and old age. In both the USA and Europe, agricultural prices were kept high by governments either paying farmers to cut production or buying up their excess products at a guaranteed price.

Post-war prosperity seemed an impressive achievement to most people who had lived through the Depression. By the 1960s, virtually full employment had come to seem normal and older people looked back with some amazement at the hardships they had endured in the 1930s.

Echoes of the past

In the 1970s and 1980s, however, mass unemployment returned and the neat story of the 'Depression defeated' was spoiled. Confusingly, leading economists once more argued that governments should cut spending and balance their budgets – exactly the view that had seemed to be discredited in the 1930s. The new trend of government policies in the 1980s and 1990s was towards cutting back on welfare and abolishing government subsidies to agriculture. In the USA, most of the legacy of the New Deal was dismantled.

Nonetheless, at the start of the new millennium the Crash of 1929 and the Great Depression were still remembered with fearful awe, as a reminder to all people of how fragile prosperity could be and how sudden the descent into economic disaster.

Present-day visitors to the Roosevelt Memorial in Washington DC pose alongside sculptures of unemployed workers of the 1930s. Could that degree of economic misery ever return to major industrial societies?

DATE LIST

1918   First World War leaves a legacy of economic instability, war debts and reparations demands.

1923   Hyperinflation in Germany destroys the value of the Deutsche Mark.

1924   In the USA, a phenomenal rise in share prices begins, initially justified by a booming economy.

1926   A General Strike is called in Britain, in support of coalminers resisting wage cuts.

1928   In Germany, unemployment begins to rise as American investment is withdrawn.

1929   Dictator Joseph Stalin initiates the first Soviet Five-Year Plan, aimed at rapid industrialization.

March   Herbert Hoover is inaugurated as president of the USA.

3 September   A sharp downturn in share prices on Wall Street marks the end of the stock market boom.

24 October   'Black Thursday': share prices crash on the US stock market.

29 October   'Black Tuesday': the worst single day of the stock market crash.

1930   Unemployment in the USA rises to 5 million.

June   The Smoot-Hawley tariff blocks the import of many agricultural goods into the USA.

1931   Three million people are unemployed in Britain, and over five million in Germany.

May   Collapse of the Kreditanstalt bank in Austria triggers a crisis in the banking system in Germany and throughout Central Europe. In Sweden, the army fires on trade unionists at Adalen.

August   Faced with a financial crisis, a Conservative-dominated National Government is established in Britain; despite cuts in public spending, it is forced to abandon the gold standard.

1932   The number of unemployed in the USA is over 12 million.

July   In the USA, the Bonus Army protesters are driven out of Washington DC.

November   Franklin D. Roosevelt wins a landslide victory in the US presidential elections.

1933   Nazi Party leader Adolf Hitler becomes Chancellor of Germany.

4 March   Roosevelt is sworn in as US president; in his first 100 days in office, legislation is passed that lays the basis for the New Deal.

1933-35   Dust storms sweep across the American Midwest as drought and over-farming create an ecological disaster.

| 1935 | The Roosevelt administration initiates the more radical 'second New Deal', including support for labour unions and social security measures. |

| 1936 | Left-wing Popular Front governments come to power in France and Spain; civil war breaks out in Spain. |

| October | The Jarrow March: unemployed shipbuilding workers carry out a protest march to London. |

| November | Roosevelt is elected for a second term as US president with another landslide victory. |

| 1936-37 | A wave of sit-in strikes sweeps the USA, leading to violent clashes between strikers and police. |

| 1937 | In the USA unemployment rises sharply again in the 'Roosevelt Depression'.

The Farm Security Administration is created in the USA to address the needs of the rural poor. |

| 1939, September | Second World War begins in Europe, soon leading to labour shortages instead of unemployment. |

RESOURCES

John Steinbeck's novel *The Grapes of Wrath* describes how a family of Okies migrates to California to escape the Dust Bowl, only to encounter harsh exploitation. It was made into a movie in 1940 by John Ford, with some scenes shot in actual migrant camps around LA.

The books of George Orwell are one of the most accessible ways into Britain's Depression years. *Down and Out in Paris and London* and, especially, *The Road to Wigan Pier* are recommended. Walter Greenwood's novel *Love on the Dole* is just about still readable.

J. K. Galbraith's *The Great Crash 1929* is a fascinating book that even manages to make economics interesting.

The Internet has much to offer on the Depression, especially in the USA. The best approach is to enter Great Depression in **yahoo.com**, and browse. At the Library of Congress's American Memory website, **memory.loc.gov.**, there is a comprehensive archive of Depression-era photographs taken by photographers working for the Farm Security Administration.

 Visit www.learn.co.uk for more resources

Sources for this book were:
Frederick Lewis Allen, *Only Yesterday*, Harper, 1931; Frederick Lewis Allen, *Since Yesterday*, Hamish Hamilton, 1940; Anthony J. Badger, *The New Deal*, Macmillan, 1989; Carl N. Degler, *Out of Our Past: The Forces that Shaped Modern America*, Harper Colophon, New York, 1984; J. C. Furnas, *Stormy Weather: An Informal Social History of the United States 1929-1941*, Putnam's, 1977; J. K. Galbraith, *The Great Crash, 1929*, Penguin 1998; Walter Greenwood, *There Was a Time*, Jonathan Cape, 1967; Walter Greenwood, *Love on the Dole*, Heineman Educational 1987 (first published 1933); Eric Hobsbawm, *Age of Extremes: The Short Twentieth Century 1914-91*, Michael Joseph, 1994; Godfrey Hodgson, *People's Century*, BBC Books, 1995; Paul Johnson, *A History of the Modern World*, Weidenfeld and Nicolson, 1984; Mark Mazower, *Dark Continent: Europe's Twentieth Century*, Penguin Books, 1999; Robert S. McElvaine ed., *Down and Out in the Great Depression*, The University of North Carolina Press, 1983; George Orwell, *The Road to Wigan Pier*, Penguin, 1989 (first published 1937); J. B Priestley, *English Journey*, Penguin, 1977 (first published 1934); John Stevenson, *British Society 1914-45*, Penguin, 1984; Studs Terkel, *Hard Times: An Oral History of the Great Depression*, Pantheon Books, New York, 1986; Patrick Wright, *The Village that Died for England*, Vintage, 1996; Richard Wright, *American Hunger*, Victor Gollancz, 1977; www.pbs.org.; Federal Writers' Project, Library of Congress.

GLOSSARY

budget deficit A budget deficit occurs when a government's spending is higher than its income. When a government's spending equals its income, the budget is 'balanced'.

bull market period when share prices are rising.

communism an extreme version of socialism, usually opposed to parliamentary democracy and advocating total state control of the economy.

corporate state a country in which business remains in private hands but the state exercises tight control over both employers and workers, allegedly in the national interest.

dole British term for all forms of unemployment benefit.

fascist originally referred to the political party set up by Benito Mussolini in Italy in the 1920s; then used for any similar authoritarian, militarist, anti-democratic movement.

free enterprise system under which the economy is in the hands of private individuals or companies, rather than state control or planning.

free trade allowing goods to be imported or exported without controls or duties.

hobo American word for a tramp.

Hooverville a shantytown of makeshift shacks housing the homeless – named ironically after US President Hoover.

import duty taxes imposed by governments on goods imported into their country.

labour exchange place where the unemployed registered as available for work.

liberal capitalism system under which free enterprise and free trade are the rule and state involvement in the economy is kept to a minimum.

Okies migrants from Oklahoma and other Dust Bowl states who drifted to California in search of work.

panhandler American term for a beggar.

primary producers countries that produce raw materials that are made into manufactured goods elsewhere, e.g. producers of wool rather than woollen clothing.

protectionist designed to protect a country's industry and agriculture against competition from foreign imports.

relief payment provided by the authorities to those living in poverty, especially as a result of unemployment.

reparations payments demanded of a defeated country by the victors to compensate for damage done in a war.

shares People invest in businesses by buying 'shares' in companies; these can be bought and sold on stock markets.

sit-in strike a strike in which employees occupy their place of work 24 hours a day, although they have stopped working.

socialist person who believes in reducing the inequality between rich and poor, usually through state control of major industries and other intervention by the state in the economy.

stocks another word for shares.

tariff a duty on imports.

unemployment insurance system under which workers receive benefit payments when unemployed, in return for paying contributions when in work.

veterans people who have fought in a war.

Wall Street site of the New York stock exchange.

welfare state system under which the state provides free health care, old age pensions and benefits for the poor and unemployed.

INDEX